FORMS OF PRAYER
at the
HOTEL EDISON

poems by
KEVIN BOWEN

CURBSTONE PRESS

FIRST EDITION, 1998
Copyright © 1998 by Kevin Bowen
All Rights Reserved

Printed in Canada on acid-free paper by Best Book
Manufacturers
Cover design: Chris Thorkelson

This book was published with the support of
the Connecticut Commission on the Arts, the
National Endowment for the Arts, and
donations from many individuals. We are very
grateful for this support.

Library of Congress Cataloging-in-Publication Data

Bowen, Kevin, 1947-
  Forms of prayer at the Hotel Edison : poems / by Kevin
Bowen. — 1st ed.
     p.   cm.
  ISBN 1-880684-55-1
    1. Vietnamese conflict, 1961-1975 — Poetry. I. Title.
PS3552.O862F6   1998
811'. 54—dc21   98-26218

published by
CURBSTONE PRESS   321 Jackson Street   Willimantic, CT 06226
    phone: (860) 423-5110   e-mail: curbston@connix.com
                www.connix.com/~curbston/

ACKNOWLEDGMENTS:

Grateful acknowledgment is made to the editors of the following
journals where some of these poems, some in other forms, first
appeared:
The Bloomsbury Review, "Francis", "The Galway Train"; *Compost,*
"Late Night in the City of Memory: West End"; *Massachusetts
Review*, "Driving Home"; *Ploughshares,* "Letter from the
North";*Press,* "At the Indochina Restaurant", "A Guest of the
Nation"; *The Progressive,* "Forms of Prayer at the Hotel Edison";
Poet Lore, "Bend in the River", "Buying My Brother a Suit" ;
Quarterly West, "Breeze"; *Rafters,* "Meditation on Tue Tinh",
"Eighty Butterfield Orchard"; *Silverfish Review,* "In Search of
Maturin", "A Little Fire: Mourning the Death of Mountbatten"; *Tar
River Poetry,* "Roses"; *Witness,* "Snapshots from LZ Julie", "The
Sandhaulers at Hue", "A Granite Stairway, St. Joseph's School for
Boys."

"Driving Home", "Father Segadeli Says Seven O'clock Mass at St.
Joseph's", "Forms of Prayer at the Hotel Edison", "Ft. Dix, New
Jersey, 1968", "Francis", "In Search of Maturin", "Inchemekinna",
and "Scalloping" appeared in *Tracks 11,* Dedalus Press, Dublin,
1996. "Sunday at the Minaun" and "Because We Were Not Home"
appeared in a special edition chapbook, *In Search of Grace
O'Malley,* published by Curbstone Press.

Special thanks to the many friends who have supported this work,
to Taylor Stoehr, George Evans, Martín Espada, Carolyn Forché,
Yusef Komunyakaa, Ralph Timperi, Nguyễn Ba Chung, Gloria
Emerson and the many friends at the Joiner Center Writers
Workshop. In Ireland, to my family, to Tom Griffin and Bríd,
Aoine, Frank, John, and Michael Neville in Dublin; to Padraig and
Mary Anne Griffin and Máire and Joe Colman McDonogh in
Carraroe; to the late Mick Neville and Michael Griffin, my guides
and to Winnie Fenton, always. Also to many friends in Viet Nam
and to Bruce Weigl, for his friendship and generosity always. Most
to my family, and to Leslie, Myles, and Lily who make it happen.

For my father and mother, and for Brian, my brother

contents

I

II

III

Forms of Prayer at the Hotel Edison

I

We are poor passing facts,
warned by that to give
each figure in the photograph
his living name.

Robert Lowell, *Epilogue*

At the Indochina Restaurant

I think of the boy today
on his cyclo at Hoàn Kiếm,
driving the carcasses of two pigs
by the lake to market.
Their flesh so pink and white,
the way he pedaled so carefully,
as if not to disturb them.
Here, all the brass fixtures,
the Australian psychiatrist
at the next table.
It is so nice to see you people returning,
we will need your help.
The waiters wear tuxedos,
serve us snake alcohol.
A young woman presses her fingers
deep into my arm,
wishes me good luck,
her regards for my family.
Outside in the rain,
her shadow is digging a tunnel.

Hà Nội, 1995

Driving Home

Out all night drinking
but not drunk.
Sent home by friends,
the round yellow pill
still on my tongue.

The car swings out
into the deep blue light,
wet splatter
of tire and asphalt.

Across the hills,
a thousand miles to Georgia.
McQuiston that June,
Caspar in fall,
just back from the jungle,
a blue truck flying
into brown mesas.

Is this what it's like?

I was running the hills
of Ohio when
my brother went off the road.
I watched a herd of deer
rush out from the woods
run right up to me
then veer off again
into the forest.

For a moment I thought
I was running with them,
hoofs just missing my feet,
their sweet moss blackened breath.

So close, I could have given
them names.

Snapshots from LZ Julie

After the passing of an arm or a leg,
who cleans up the mess?

Where are their maps?

No, this picture is not a picture of men.
Show us again.

And this man's heart.
Who will return it to its rightful place?

Read me their names.
The ones who were there.

And the ones who sent them.

Where are their pictures?

Not in these boxes,
these are old friends.

Kiss them now.
I ask you.

Kiss these arms,
this leg,
this heart.

Now bury
them.

Learning Code: Ft. Gordon, Georgia, 1968

Lightning shimmers in the East.
Signals distant storms.

Inside the long tin huts
it's the humidity that gets them.

So many this year:
boys hooked up to earphones,

waiting strange messages to come.

Fort Dix, New Jersey, February 1968

Morning's cold, gray winds
blow down barren ranges.
Teenage boys huddle and hug
the hard New Jersey earth.

One more time today, they fire
rifles from frozen holes,
helmets knocking,
watch on knolls for silhouettes,
the almost human targets,
who rise and fall.

Five miles out, and back snow-lined roads,
coffee and potatoes heaped from metal drums,
planes drone overhead.

In Asian villages women wake to mourning.
Monks of Thiên Mụ flee to the forests.

Guard Duty, Biên Hoà, 1968

He was just another soldier,
lonely in a bunker.
When a friend offered love
he took it,
and gave it back again.

His one mistake, to tell the sergeant;
his face a raw-boned sea
after that, the small red fish
we watched swim by
in the oceans of his eyes.

And then the chaplain,
who heard his confession,
but not the snap of the clip
when he crawled back into the bunker.

Men tunnel through the earth
all around us, looking for love.

No one sleeps anymore.

ARVNS

What were their chances anyway?
The two of us went through them
like a village of scared children
pushing, barking out orders,
sent them on through the gate,
sure they took nothing,
only the memory of our faces,
our fathers' watches
bleeding like moons from our eyes.

West of Tây Ninh

We walked straight into the forests of the dying,
night fires still burning on the hills.
Each man carried another on his back.
A woman with one leg balanced a child on her lap.
One man asked for radios.
No one apologized.
We felt the hum of the blades from the lumber yard
calling us back.
Someone passed a cup filled with fireworks.
We lit them in our mouths.
We sang the forbidden songs.

Casualties II

This one, he
sits out in the car
off the highway.
Life goes on
but he can't see
the glaze of salt
that plays on the wind.
I still go round and round
its traces.
This one, he died of exposure.
The last time I saw him,
just back from the war,
he and his father
fighting like strangers.
My friend wanted to
roll a grenade
into the bar where he
worked running tables.
He was crazy back then.
They were rich college kids.
It wasn't their fault,
I told him.
He stood outside
calling to them
before he disappeared too
through the war's window.
It's not him. It's not him,
his father kept saying
at the wake.
Some things so
far beyond
pain there
is no language.

Sailing to Thái Bình

Who would have thought so much cold
this far south? Early morning, we drive
Route Five, the great wide mouth
of the Red River opening out before us.
Dark brown fields hang in the mist,
stretch to the vanishing point.
The farmers who work them have bent
their thin bodies already for hours to earth.
They wear red bandannas around their necks,
bundle for warmth in the rhythm
of flood and mud and rain,
planting the last winter rice.
Three centuries since men and women
cut out a road from here to drag
a new bell for Keo Pagoda.
They labored so hard to set it gently in the wooden tower
high above the lily pond,
last carved their names in bronze, then turned,
foot by foot to cover the road over again.
Thirty nine stones in the temple well,
each one knocked hollow hammering
grain to feed the workers.
From here the French hung bodies
as warnings by the side of the road,
lifted whole villages to the mountains.
From here Bui Viện picked up his small bundle,
walked the long road south,
sailed a year around the world,
to step into Tyler's office,
beg him to send the French away.
From here a boy crossed from a buffalo's back,
looked down at his fields from the moon.

Letter from the North

for B.W. and P.T.D.

In wet fields the farmers' cramped
hands clutch fast to their hoes.
We tumble through stone-colored flesh.
All night the plane floating up over the oceans,
unknown lives passing through us.
So many. Barely enough time to say the names.
Gone, as if taken by a huge gray
hand entering a station, or those boats
with makeshift heads
nosing the stairs by the river.
This morning I turned the corner at Bùi Thị Xuân
and walked into a funeral. The great black
bus without doors sailed past me,
the white banded mourners, red flags
leading drummers to the lake.
What is it we have seen
that we must travel so far to pray?

On Mai Hắc Đế last night
I sat with the old men
in the slow dripping rain
and watched the cards fall in the dark.
Someone called my name,
I turned too late.
The gate creaked closed, a shadow
moving in the smoke of the kerosene lamp.
Outside the Apocalypse Bar, tourist buses
lined up on their way to the snake restaurant.
A young girl and her brother huddled in jackets
over a charcoal fire. They offered their warmth for sale.
A wooden bench, brandy, Laotian tobacco, strong tea.

Mutes, I sat and watched them sign in the darkness,
faces screwed up into those unsayable syllables,
bodies twisting, arms turned up, bent like ancient
wrestlers or those gods carved on old temple ceilings,
or the hump-backed man, two birds on his shoulders
by the yellow wall at Trấn Quốc Pagoda.
On Hàng Vải St., the wedding procession
stopped to light fireworks.
In the narrow street of restaurants, rockets
flew up in the air, drawing whole families out
to see the hissing snakes' heads of the flares,
the green and yellow sparks falling on tin rooftops.
Bà Chúa Liễu, she came in a red dress first.
At her shrine I watched a soldier
burn money in a pit for his lost companions.
Time, he said. That's all.
In the story everyone already knew
the young girl was Lan Cô, the old King's daughter.
The third time she came she was dressed in white at
                                                    Hồ Tây.
This is what my friend told me in the small boat
that took us there, boat rocking in the misty waters,
the early morning fog, the great fields of birds spread
like beggars fingers calling from the lake.
Oh my friends, If they keep coming
I think their shadows will make a bridge
even our poor souls could cross.

Phố Hai Bà Trưng

At the pagoda of the sisters
two women in brown suits
count out the day's receipts.

From bright red curtains
a white horse peers out behind them,
his paint so slowly peeling.

The old men on the steps
flap their arms as if
to fend off the bad weather,

their pockets stuffed with camellias.
On the street by the lake,
rows of women slake mud

washed up from storms,
mist rising off their backs.
So beautiful, you can almost see

the old gods descending,
curling up into the exact
ends of their fingertips.

Meditation on Tuệ Tĩnh

Four AM.
Two old women

alone on the street.
Their words fall off

to traffic sounds behind them.
A boy turns the corner,

a small black dog
beside him.

They disappear
back into darkness.

Silence.
Whir of a bicycle.

First scrape of tables
pulled out to pavement.

Clack of knives
slammed down on wood.

The first phở shops opening.
Soft clipped words of greeting.

More women arriving.
Arranging themselves in a circle.

A market
at the edge of the curb.

The Sandhaulers at Huế

All day they labor,
their backs stretched
like canvas in the sun,

black shirts open, soaked
with sweat and river water.
They take turns only to rest

at the rudder, a single oar
set in a rough wooden tongue.
They seem almost unaware

how their loads change color,
black to blue to white.
Standing so still,

like runes on the waters,
moving so gently
to sweep their long oars

past the fields of white lilies,
those long armed swimmers,
that rise in the currents.

They turn their heads then
so slightly, as if trying to listen,
deep at the bottoms,

the roots in their tangles,
struggling to lift
the heads of the flowers free.

March, 1995. Twentieth anniversary of Liberation

Bend in the River

Late afternoon sun,
mountains,
miles of wet fields,
an illusion of mirrors.

The Bàng tree's first leaves
just turning yellow.
Tourists eat pommes frites
by the bridge where a thousand died.

Gray boats slip past
on their way to market,
temple,
white sands of a cemetery.

Darkness crawls up,
down river,
lamps lit to draw fish,
starred nets dropping.

Let us in, let us in, the dead call.

Their hands reach up.
Their hands reach up.

The Poetry Garden at Sông Bé

"I hear my village calling me through the
eyes of the cracked leaves."
                                      Nguyễn Duy

He bends the candle to the book so I can see.
I fight to find the words of the poem.
Nine times through the course of the war
he moved.
The last time he stopped,
he built this house of stone.

Twenty miles out from the city
we sit in the fading light
at the edge of the jungle
in the poetry garden.

Three cemeteries surround us,
the dead of three different wars.
Their voices are the crickets' cries tonight.
They make a chorus for the young woman,
her face so sad, so beautiful,
who sings by the empty chair.

Her long thin fingers drop like buddhas,
spread and lift the gray wet hairs
that fall and cling across her temple.

Over and over, she repeats
the words of the refrain.

Chiến Tranh, Chiến Tranh.
The war is no joke.

The bonfire burns, specks of fire
break off and crack and circle
the garden on the hill.
They rise like incense in the night.

The crickets' cries grow louder.
The frogs begin their harsh calling from the trees.
Who knows where a thing leaves off?
Some one always telling a story.

This one of sunlight falling away into a tree line,
an intricate architecture of paths
through rubber trees.

How far they had come.
How that afternoon his friend
had bent and lifted
the lid of his past
and a hand had reached up,
held out to him a piece of shining metal.

*Con chết. Con chết, t*he buffalo boy
with the dark brown eyes had cried
and run screaming from the bunker,
then the hand from the past reaching up
to take it all so fast away.

Chiến Tranh. Chiến Tranh.
The war is no joke.

In the poetry garden faces disappear
and reappear in the flickering light.
Where is the child who has run away?
The one left behind in the highlands?
The Cải Lương singer bends her face low over her lover,
her song is a cool wave riding out on the night.

Her two friends take her hands and hold them,
squeeze them tight to their breasts,
as if to take the sadness of the song
back into their hearts
and save her,
save us all.

Meditation at Từ Hiếu Pagoda

For Thích Thiện Hạnh

In the courtyard, the Mai trees pruned back.
A few spare leaves, one yellow flower.

Beneath them, roses curl
in earthen pots.

At the meditation house,
bowls of rice set out.

Đại trees, white limbs,
pressed home to heaven.

A single monk walks
down the trail.

His legs disappear
in blue paddy water.

II

History Lessons

for C.A. O'Connor

They say our history is the history
of bones,

the history of tall men and women,
sheer brown cliffs and birds.

They say our history is the history
of fog down the pass,

of clouds on the mountain,
taste of sweet malt and grass.

They say our history is the history
of creak of wood,

of grain of boat underfoot,
history of foxglove and steeplebush,

stone church and tower,
history of men singing in circles,

women fingering cloth and beads,
history of spear by the fire,

of long fish smoking and turf-
hardened backs.

They say our history is the history of hunger,
history of secrets at crossroads,

of insult and vendetta,
history of fosterage and parricide,

history of curses.
They say our history is the history

of the too great love of saints
and of shop girls,

of seed on the ground
and dropping faces.

They say our history is the history
of riverbeds and their sources,

of monks in cells,
and trout in cold waters.

They say our history is the history
of lists, of long genealogies,

names of dark ships,
and men and woman who sailed them.

They say our history is the history
of late night lies and morning betrayals,

the history of slow fuses and phone calls,
of decapitations and car bombs.

They say our history is as
simple as this.

Our history is the history
of our words.

Our history is the history
of our deeds.

Our history is the history
of our silences.

Sunday at the Minaun

Bobby Sands picture above the bar,
the green white scarf draped over his too young face.

In Kinshasa last night, two hundred killed.
In the morning paper a photo of a rebel in an alley

shooting one of Mobuto's sad-faced soldiers.
How many know why they fight?

In the North whispers of peace talks,
of how the parties will meet at a secret location

but will not have to speak.
Minaun looking down. The goat, in Irish.

I too once prayed for a miracle, but all I got
was a red chair moving across the room,

a newspaper opening its pages
to all the wrong answers.

Fregan. Answer.
Tomorrow the Chinese take back Hong Kong.

But still the Tutsi's have nowhere to go. Their hungry,
dying faces linger in the low light of the bar.

Sunday rains driving the families in:
parents and children seeking shelter after mass.

So little light. Yesterday, the sheep looked at me
as if there was something I should know.

The lambs flitting back and forth across the road.
So far away, everything happening

as if through the lens of a slow motion camera.
As if all love had gone out of the world.

Caladh Thadagh

If in this gutted house I still could pray
I would ask her to come back, come back
to this small house by the sea,
I would ask her to come back and hold me,
rock me, lay my head down one more time
on the cold floor, its dirt still damp
with the making of whiskey.
I would ask her to bring me back with her,
let me hold them as they turn in the night,
search for the missing place beside them,
let me reach in to touch them in all
the places their bodies have been wasted.
I would ask her to let me huddle with them
those days the winds blow in, rain
breaking their backs like a sacrament,
to let me pick up and put on their clothing
as they lay naked making love,
one eye out for the children,
the scent of fish and turf still kissing them
in its blanket. I would ask her to let me
fall with them nights in their drunkenness,
let me walk with them up the hill
to the church in the morning, sing with them
the thick consonants, rough vowels.
I would ask her to let me feel with them
the anger of the rifle butt deep in the shoulder,
sit up with them nights of their planning,
whisper with them the names of the ships
they'll never return on.

The Galway Train

At the Dublin Station,
the high rise and fall of arms.

Friday night, everyone
headed home for the holidays.

I was lost until three women
from the islands found me

and took me. They knew already
where I was going,

sat me in the berth beside them,
tried to teach me the words

I'd need to get there.
Three hours, the smoke

slowly taking over the car,
endless fields out the window.

A deep, bone-dug knot letting go.
Picture of a woman reading a newspaper by a fire:

"Farm Prices Falling."
Corners of the page folding in.

Inchemekinna

I never asked how it was that when the Hunger came
they all went to the island;
or how they could survive on that small slip
of broken rock and green,
only a quarter mile across, a half mile long.
Never a good place to land a boat;
no sure footing.
Southwest, looking to the Arans, the single high point,
no more than twenty feet above the tide.
A few low, sloping trees.
But all around the island's waist
the kelps' rocky harvest, the razor necks,
shells rising up like white, speckled hands
to draw the gulls and birds
whose leavings made the beds deep and safe,
sent the flowers crawling up in terraces
the whole eastern side of the island.
The houses abandoned now,
chimneys crushed,
five, counting the one I stand in.
The shadow of its fires still black
against the back room wall,
the room where Brid, the last to die here, was waked,
long lines of men and women
sailing in from Gorumna, Lettermore, and Spiddal,
wet scarves dripping up the path all afternoon.

A Guest of the Nation

At the blacksmith's house at Caladh Thadagh
I couldn't understand the red arm returning,
the clip moving back and forth in fire,
the hiss of the waters; or further down the road
the old men in the pub speaking Irish and pointing.
The shooters and beer had started there
with Padraig and Joe Coleman.
Whiskey, "The Green Spot," from Kildare St.
But then we were off, past the wall
where the man had gone off the road
the week before. Poteen, they said.
We turned up to the house to buy some,
then drove off for the docks
to check the boats for morning,
stepping in and out, in and out, over the gunnels,
flicking cigarettes into the wind.
Two more pubs after that.
Flaherty's and Concannons.
Men rising like saints from chairs.
Everyone a cousin.
I wanted to marry a girl with dark hair and a red sweater
and may have proposed or bought a house on the island
before they took me home to more cousins,
a field of arms helping me upstairs,
the hot water bottle,
tucking me in with the children,
the baby in his cradle
looking down at my head
all giggles and coos in the morning.

Scalloping: Carraroe West

Three figures in a long black currach
steer south into a January morning.
In the stillness, they stop to smoke;
two men and a boy, old family trade.
The tall man stands, draws up
a long ash pole, swings wide-spiked
teeth out from the gunwales,
slides them deep into the blue waters,
starts to sweep the sea bed.
One by one he eyes the sleeping
crusted hands come to life,
scuttle across the ocean floor.
Back-wrenching work, their bodies
steam in dulled half-light,
push up and down the shore.
Dusk, catch spills over quaking floorboards.
Home at nightfall, shells bake
over turf, a fire centuries old.
A boy with eager hands
cuts the first one open,
shows his guest the secret:
the thick red lips of the scallop.

In Search of Maturin

We will see you if you come.
    —The Maturin Sisters

Past the Hellfire club, the thin man
runs down the road from the Dublin mountains,
makes the hum of a motorcycle
the state says he's too mad to drive,
takes a whole lane to himself,
stopping traffic before him,
everyone turning back to see.

Aungier St., a candle burns,
the back room at St. Peter's.
He bends over a table that will end
in the madhouse at Grangegorman
because he's in debt again.
This time they will take all of the furniture.
Only the bare walls left, the lush murals,
scenes from his novels. Melmoth on the beach.

One hundred fifty poor interments this year.
This formerly prosperous but now impoverished city.

Each day, up Redmonds Hill,
Bishop St., White Friars, back to St. Peters.
What if in a city there were a castle
and a theater, and people hung, pale bodies
pulled down, drawn and quartered
in front of their homes, Emmet,
and in the bone kitchens
families waiting the nightly carnival of their hunger.

Already I hear the rabble of saints in the streets.

A candle burns. Three AM Laudanum.
Paste a wafer to your head. Await inspiration.

*We wake and wonder at the delusion under which we
toiled.*

A man in this city once stopped me
and told me before I ever asked
that no, there had never been men
up there on that moon he pointed to,
only horses circling a tower in the desert.
All sandstorms, he said.

Later, two children
grabbed my arms
to greet me
and picked my pockets clean
and when I realized what they'd done,
I went off to chase them,
"Cause, Christ," the cop on the beat said,
"I'm too slow and fat to,"

and when I caught them,
cornered them on the bridge
where the crowd gathered,
those two children
got down on their knees
and pleaded,
"Jesus, Mary and Joseph, Mister,
Please don't beat us."
No, no fault in madness here.

In the picture
you stand in the small green yard, right arm
draped over Michael's shoulder.
He wears a steel blue suit.
First Communion Day.
The Dublin Mountains
climb up over your heads.
A field of fresh-planted pine.
Brid leans beside you, cracking
only a hint of a smile.
Who knew what was coming down
so fast upon us.
I left you standing at the ferry.
Later the letter came.
You had started the treatments.
You would not be coming on with the delegation.
I sat up thinking of the children.
There is no kind country for the dying.
What more was there to say?

For Mick Neville

Famine Stew

Another Sunday, he climbs the winding stairs to visit
my grandmother. All afternoon, they will sip whiskey
and tea by the window, trade stories of Churchill and
Cromwell, — their Neolithic hunger for the Irish.
She will recall the texture of each loss, the slow
slipping away that came with each small progress.
Their faith. The language. He will recite the names of
the families who left, the ones who remained, year
after year, all the way back to The Famine.
Only there do they reach their stride, his low voice
rasping in anger: how the Quaker ships, loaded with
grain for the dying, were held up, forced
to pay the British tariffs. How a man had to sell
off his land, all but a quarter acre, to get
the assistance; then the family forced
to build the narrow roads leading to nowhere
— Famine Roads, lest they become indolent.
Famine Stew. He knew the recipe by heart.
To six gallons of water add four ounces of beef,
carrots and turnips as wanted. Made with
the counsel of the best doctors and chefs
in Europe. And the rich, yes the rich,
he remembered the stories: how they
put on disguises, dressed in old tweeds,
rubbed their hands in the ditches,
snuck into the lines just to try it.

A Little Fire: Mourning the Death of Mountbatten, Dublin, January, 1978

In Dublin, I saw twelve men in dark blue suits
line the porcelain wall of a bar, pissing.
They could have been volunteers
from a high school drill team
the way they shook out their penises
with such precision,
talked on in mid-afternoon calm.
Inside the bar, three old men near ninety
sat bent at a table, drinking.
Above their heads,
on a TV screen, the ten-gallon
hats of cowboys yahooed a dinosaur
into a wooden cathedral in a movie
where now church and dinosaur
both were burning.
" A little fire," one turned and smiled,
"is good for us all once and a while."

A March for the Repatriation of Irish Prisoners from English Jails, Oxford, 1979

for Tom Griffin

We were marching up St. Aldates,
recounting the dark history
of our miseries,
the old lexicon of torture.
We should have known better.
Near the theater, the skinheads started
throwing stones and swearing.
The police steered us off.
At first we thought for out own protection
until we turned the narrow street
into the cul de sac, blind alley, dead end,
we knew so well,
the sun hanging high in the bough
of the single tree above us,
the slow arc of the rocks.
Cops laughing,
"friggin Irish."

Broad St. Riots

for Patrick Bohannon

On June 11, 1837, Boston firefighters ran through an
Irish funeral procession. A battle between firefighters
and mourners spread until militia were called to put
down the disturbance.

Maybe they could have stopped the procession,
or moved a little faster to let the engines pass.
The kind mud at their feet.
'Their strange exotic ways.'

When the rioters ran out of bricks,
they climbed back up Broad St.
to the tenements,
tore their mattresses up
threw fistfuls of feathers down
into the burning streets.

Days later, the warrants followed.
Men seen heading westward in the night.
Recruits for the hard riding armies.
Later, Santa Anna's "red companies"
at Buena Vista, Churubusco, Chapultepec:
The San Patricios.

Eighty Butterfield Orchard

So slowly the light arrives here.
A body can turn for hours waiting
the sun. This is the city gave gray
its name. So cold the way the winds
blow up the Military Road, curl past
the mountains and low-cupped fields
of the old artillery ranges, past the small
brook and hills, the stone church
where yesterday I shuffled my feet back and forth,
adjusted my coat, as the priest went on
and on of the evils of fornication. The young
just shook their heads; outside, they broke
in packs, like starlings on the bay, heads
bent to the broken lines of cement,
the spray-painted graffiti ... *Smash H Block.*
Each day I ride the five miles in to the city,
watch the smokers climb to the top of the bus
like penitents. At dusk, I cross Kildare St.,
collect my few small beers, wake near dawn
in the small room at the back of the house,
staring up to the lintel, the slow uncertain
handwriting. *Colm McDonogh came here,*
1961. My grandmother's brother, who never left.
What was he thinking when he wrote this
I wonder. In his granddaughter's house.
So far from the West. Maybe he was just
a little drunk, as I have been. I try to imagine
his hand that night, as he reached into his pocket
for the knife, struggling with his one good arm
to push himself up from the bed, feel for the fresh
grain of the lintel, set the knife deep into its notches,
carve out one simple message that would last.

Because We Were Not Home

for Winnie and Peggy

When you came by we were out
following the shepherd as he
climbed the rock cliffs at Keel.
He was leading his sheep up
the path by the falls, walking
them one by one as if he were
leading them into some picture
or painting. His small white dog
ripped and cut at their heels,
pushed them deep up
in line along the brown slope.
They moved together as if
under one of those glass spheres
you place on the mantle.
We climbed through wet moss
and rock, looking to find the high
ground, cut back and forth
across the nubs and rivulets,
trying to find the cutbacks to the old paths.
Half-way up, when we turned
we saw the sunlight like a beacon
slipping down from the clouds
onto the cold turquoise sea,
the sheep fields washed in its yellow light,
the soft greens and whites, the red door
of Michael Carr's house, his blue-eyed dogs
run wild in the yard.
What we thought a cemetery
was only another sheep field
at the top of a hill. We walked
the long path back, the children

threw rocks along the beach,
too late we found your note under the door.
Sorry we missed you, it said –
driving all the way from Carraroe
to let us know the phones
were out, you were leaving on Sunday,
hoped we would be enjoying our stay.

A Picture from the Island

for Tómas Griffin

The picture he hands me, it is one of those nameless
pictures,the people in them long forgotten.
There are six of them in the photo: two men lean
loosely at attention against the white-washed walls
of a farm house. Two women, their wives, sit
stiffly in front, in chairs outside the cottage.
A boy maybe ten, his mouth open, is just turning
to look to the camera. He is dressed
in a wool sweater and jacket.
Another boy is just entering the house by the door,
his back turned, as he crosses the threshold.
The men wear tweed caps. They are tall and thin,
dressed for cold weather in homespun shirts,
old sweaters, jackets. The women bend slightly,
they huddle in dresses and shawls.
These are the last inhabitants of the island.
This, the last picture of them taken together.
In six months the men will be dead, the women
forced to take over their boats until bad weather
and poor health force them to pack up
and leave off the island.
Bríd, the woman in the center,
she will be the last to die there.
Six of them, they stare back to the camera,
posed for a sister gone to America.
Come, they say. Your flesh and blood.
Look at us. See how we miss you. Remember us,
for this world will never see our like again.

III

Breeze

I can't stop the heat from coming
or the window from jamming.
I prop it up with a book to let in
what's left of the breeze when it gets here.
Five floors up, two windows over,
the mailman dreams himself home
drunk again, the sound of the slaps
covering his wife's body pass
through the leaves in the trees
on their way to the river.
A voice yells up to be quiet.
Old man Newell's car sits at the end
of the alley like a deflated blue corpse,
his son with no arms to dig himself out
of the shallow grave on the hill in Korea.
City of the unreturning.
My brother takes my arm,
places in the center of my palm
a white handkerchief he will tie
on his head like a bandanna
then run out to the street,
a mad, barking dog, his one aim
to drive the organ grinder's sad
brown monkey to a deep and holy distraction.
His beatific smile passing under
the walls' of the great stone jail,
the clock at its top telling the wrong time
as rain washes dirt down the street,
and tiny rivulets of white and black
sand and salt scribble messages
by brown square patches of trees
that never grow,

and still the sun rises to bleed
all day into the hill,
window after window stretching
to breathe the thinning air,
release the tired words of old families
praying in old languages.
Prayers for special intentions,
for the sick and dying, a release
from pain, a son's return,
the conversion of neighbors.
Prayers rising up through the trees
of the honeycombed heart
of the deep- tunneled city,
falling over dancers falling out
of the rooming houses onto
the avenues of oncoming boys,
one with a knife in his pocket,
the red tip of a cigarette cupped
in his hands, the vision ahead
of a ship going down, smell
of potato and cabbage, green linoleum,
a Formica table in the projects,
above which a man lifts,
is lifting, and kissing
a boy because his brother is born today
and it is hot and it is raining.

Urban Renewal

I have a friend
in the city, his office
twenty stories up
from where his house
once stood.
He had to quit, he said,
he couldn't take
the sadness.
Like a young boy
who puts his hand
in the river
and feels the small fish
rush to his fingers
he felt his past
swimming all around him.
He said if he listened
he heard the wind
carrying the voices
of the dead strippers and boxers
up to his window.
Nights when he left
he could smell the old city of flophouses,
the cheap restaurants:
Billy Boys, Joe & Nemo's —
the Hot Dog Kings, the Aragon.
Sometimes in meetings
he said he'd drift off,
see himself a boy again
leaning up Bowdoin St., Bobby Smith
smashing the glass moon
of the Hotel Earl one more time,
Johnny Wu's father

at the door of his laundry
waving his fist.
In a screen of blue
smoke, when his boss
was talking,
once, he said he saw
his grandmother
dancing in the darkness
of the hallway
with that sweet man
Bela Lugosi.

Late Word in the City of Memory: West End

For F.X. J.

When the derricks
move in single file up the street
and the garbage burns blue
under your window, know
soon it will be time to leave.

In the days that remain
memorize names,
house by house, block by block.
The Burke's here, the Fitzgerald's there.
The Capadalupo's and the Pasqua's.

And in the procession to the church
who played John the Baptist,
who spat in whose eye,
and what politician
swore at whose mother
simply for raising her fist
to the man who tore down her house,
and every house around it,
left a vacant lot of rubble
forty acres wide, only
the streetlights still standing.

Uncle

Uncle you must have done a lot of thinking
floating out there in the ocean.
Speke went mad looking for the source of the Nile,
you lay there three days bobbing in the sea,
staring at the dead hills of Africa.
You probably didn't even exist to the German
commander who was most likely thinking
of his wife back home
when he whispered the order to fire,
then set himself for the jolt
of torpedoes.
And you, were you in your hammock, or up
on deck smoking? You never said.
Eighteen years old and all those faces
going down around you.
When they plucked you from the water
they sent you to a camp
in the middle of the country,
which was good enough for you,
a man like Ulysses
who never wanted again to know
the briny green smell of the oceans.
The rest of your life, seeing it
happen over and over again,
as others explained what it meant.
At the museum last week
I saw the Mayan tapestries
hanging from the walls.
They say men sailed the oceans,
climbed the Andes, traded gold
and feathers of rare birds
for the stories woven there.

I thought of you, uncle, when I saw
the one with the mountains, the oceans
and sharks. They say the Mayans
took the best and burned them for the gods,
or buried them deep in caves,
then threw the weavers in.

Love in the Days of the Strangler

All that year their bodies fell and fell
until they made a circle.
The old Polish widow on Grove St.
over Nick the Tailor's,
the nurse on Charles St.
by the Paramount Cafe.
This much I remember —
the front hall door was open,
the living room sofa pulled out into the bed
where my sisters had been sleeping.
Through the kitchen,
in the single bedroom,
two plainclothesmen were questioning my mother.
She was showing them the drawer
from where he must have
pulled the clothing out
before kneeling down beside her,
how long she didn't know.
At first, she thought it was a dream,
or one of the children;
then, paralyzed, unable to scream,
moved her hand slowly
to the other side of the bed,
to our father.
Here the world drops off to silence.
Outside, no sirens scream,
the green lamp posts burn through the window,
their dull yellow glow.
Just us in that old brick house,
her mother's house,
standing there, staring at her.
She is so young.

Something in her face tells me
I will never know what she's thinking,
her left hand clutching tight to the sheet,
holding off in the night
the half-rising voices
of the strangled dead.

A Granite Stairway: St Joseph's School for Boys

So many lives pressed into stone.
No vacant moments but always the praying,
praying for the right words to come.
For forgiveness. Always, the Nine AM
rush of cassocks along the rails,
boys off to mass and funerals.
Afternoons, air raid drills,
cold dark walls against legs,
dreaming the flash of the bomb,
the heavy tomb like quiet,
a litany of names called into darkness:
Jackman, Kussy, Macaroni,
Bedugnis, Fitzgibbon, Pienisuski,
Salvator Bordinaro.
Boys whose fathers
worked at the post office,
bakery, track, the shoe store.
Boys down on their knees
praying for the war not to come,
for Russia's conversion.
Boys stepping off into a gray mist
to lead the procession each spring,
listening one more time
to the story of a girl in France,
and three children in Portugal,
who'd seen the Virgin;
and of one who carried a message to the Pope
who had yet to reveal its secret.

Father Segadeli Says Seven O'Clock Mass at St. Joseph's

We kneel in the cold wooden pews
of the basement church of St. Joseph's.
Father Segadeli is lost again.
Somewhere between Lombardy and Korea
he has left us.
Maybe it was a noise from in the back
of the church that set him off,
but now he is off, lost somewhere
between the Mass of the Communicants
and the Mass of the Faithful.
Soon his six-foot-nine-inch frame,
hunched over the tabernacle,
rises in a low moan.
He moves back from the altar,
knows he must say the words as they were given.
Et Introibo ad altare dei.
He begins the mass again.
I will go unto the altar of god.
No one leaves.

Francis

The children found you, Christmas morning.
The far corner of the park.
Two days you lay there,
the voice on the radio said,
behind the abandoned Buick,
your body set on fire half a dozen times
before it finally caught.
A man wearing a dress.

Too soon the old words rolling off the tongue.
Faggot. Homo. Queen.
Sunday mornings
we watched you stroll to the altar,
bleached hair tossed back, like Monroe's in *The Misfits*.
Your face made-up in mascara, false lashes,
you held your chin forward like a gift.
We waited wondering would you fall,
the host sear off your tongue.

Whatever burned inside you, Francis,
they felt they needed a fire to kill.
In the snow your struggle left a black star.

The Gypsies at St. Patrick's

It was late at night or after wakes
my father told the story of how
in New York, after the war,
the gypsies had first appeared
at the Cathedral, how Sundays,
they slipped into the communion
lines, heads bowed in mock
devotion, knelt beneath the priest,
their tongues rolled out in innocence,
waiting to take and tuck the host
inside a cheek. Then a slow turn,
their shoulders hunched as they
picked up speed to the rear of the church,
the sudden, wild laughter, someone
swearing – Gypsies – the chase
to the streets where they spit the wafers out,
stomped them into the pavement
as the first wave of men from church
pulled them back into a halo of arms
and the second dove to shovel
the bleeding hosts back into their mouths.

Forms of Prayer at the Hotel Edison

Last days before the war,
midnight, the end of his shift,
I watch him step out from the darkness
under the hotel canopy
into the streetlight's glare.
Night clerk in a dying city.

I know his feet must ache, standing all night,
watching the prostitutes, junkies, cops.
Some nights I think I see tears in his eyes,
maybe from the cold,
or a gas release from the chemical plant.

When he takes his place in the front seat of the car,
I crawl over into the back to sleep on the drive home,
listen to a man on the radio say he doesn't believe
in that place where already too many are dying.
In the windshield's reflection,
I see my father's beautiful hands, praying.

Roses

All summer mint spread like a mad green drummer
parading back and forth beneath the porch
Digging up its wildness was work.
So much bending, turning old soil,
mixing fresh loam, then a moment
when his back and mine were one,
and I saw again, the dirt at the cuffs,
socks hanging down as he weeded,
picked beetles off each leaf,
dropped them in bell jars.

Caring was what mattered;
the day's work
spaced with long breaks under the maple
where he wiped his face,
caught the breath that would eventually fail
on the last first day of spring.

Now, we touch again across the roses.

Buying My Brother a Suit

In the old days they'd open the stores
on Sundays and holidays
if you called.
But today is Friday,
and I have come to buy
a suit for my brother
who never owned a suit,
my brother, who drove a cab nights
and in the day
cared for the sick and the crazy.
He would laugh if he saw me here.
But this is the way we live:
we take care of our own.
So I have come to buy my brother a suit
to slip his long arms in one last time,
blue to match his eyes.
Later tonight, after
the mourners arrive,
and the room is full,
all of us remembering
what we loved best,
I will walk up to him
to check the line of his tie,
my sisters beside me,
nodding their approval.

Brothers

That time of year again
I feel you slowly moving in my body,
blood in blood.

I look in the mirror at my nakedness,
it is your girth I see,
your eyes
looking back at me,
looking into my face,
face which my friends
tell me, each day becomes
more and more
like yours.

So beautiful,
the way we grow into
each other's bodies,
how we never really part,
but spread out into
each other's lives.

What one day I had forgotten,
one night, looking out over the river
I hear you whisper
back to me.

This year, more and more,
I have come to know
how much the dead
inhabit me,
how at night and even

in the daytime
they come to me,
bringing me poems,
nudging me,
this thing, this thing you have
forgotten.

Kabachanik

His fingers shoot six foot flowers and burning ingots.
He moves his feet and a dozen children swirl around him.
This is what comes of genius and survivors.
Soon we begin our chanting. *Kabachanik Kabachanik.*
His name like a eucharist on our lips.
Kabachanik. Kabachanik. His hands in the pockets,
his suit of a thousand flags stitched together.
But we can't help ourselves.
Kabachanik Kabachanik Someone lights a firecracker.
Kabachanik Kabachanik Someone calls from a window.
A woman's head leans from a red brick house.
He turns, moves toward us, his feet like his head,
too big for his body. *Kabachanik Kabachanik.*
His awkward lunge and swing, then
that voice like a lost Caruso rushing up the street,
those long hallways of doors opening.

For Myles Who Communes with Planes

In the backyard I hold him up.
Nine months old, already his hand slaps out

the tempo of a vicious dribble.
Basketball, his great passion,

until a plane nears overhead.
He stirs before we hear it,

flinches as if he knows it's there
before it even flies in view.

He makes a rite of its passing.
First he turns, searches the sky,

seeks the strand of light in the distance,
then waves, pours a stream of wondrous

babble. I follow his lead, search,
point and smile. But what it is he's thinking

still eludes me. Is it joy he finds
in an image? A kind and gentle

god he sees up there? Or are they
faces of souls he recognizes,

disguised, bearing familiar features
from other lives?

Does he think it some small bird
he begs to descend, to land and

rest on the outstretched finger
of the hand he points?

Or is it finally some memory
from the womb he celebrates?

A last recollection, hum and image,
the moment of his leaving, brightness,

and that first great mystery of flight?

The Connemara Woman

The Friday before you left
the old woman walked out
across the field to press
a locket to your breast.
Thirteen and you were
leaving home forever.

Sunday, you kissed your
brother Coleman good-bye,
left to walk the twenty-six
miles of winding road—
past the barrens, past the last
fields of rock and larks and sheep
to the city.

Baptised the 23rd of January, 1874.
Parish of Kileen and Gorumna.
Barbara McDonogh, daughter
of John McDonogh and Sibbona Flaherty
of Carraroe South.
Sponsors: Pat and Kate Montague.

The painter came in summer
to capture the landscape
and the people
before they disappeared.

You would never know
the soldier who pressed
you up against the wall
by the barracks where
you lost your voice was just

as young and frightened
as yourself, didn't know
you couldn't speak English,
thought like all the rest
you were hiding something.
But you were just looking to hide.

On the left wall, furthest room, deep
into the exhibit I find the painting.
You stare blindly to the distance.

You never knew your portrait hung here.
You never wanted to go back.

Now you stand barefoot at the lintel,
the lake, a pile of turf, on one side,
the bay behind.

The wind blows wet and cool
against your neck. Dogs bark,
race in pairs around the eel thick lake.
So certain of their quarry.

notes

"Fort Dix, New Jersey, February 1968": Thiên Mụ, 16th century pagoda on the Perfume river, center of Buddhist opposition to the war.

"ARVN'S": soldiers of the Army of the Republic of Vietnam (South Vietnam)

"Letter from the North" is for Bruce Weigl and Phạm Tiến Duật. The Temple of Bà Chúa Liễu is on the West Lake in Hà Nội.

"The Poetry Garden at Sông Bé" is for Thu Bồn, Nguyễn Duy, and for Bob Glassman.

"Meditation at Từ Hiếu Pagoda": Từ Hiếu Pagoda, located in the hills of Huế, is home to the Liệu Quan School of Buddhism, the temple of Thích Nhạt Hạnh, poet and activist, who now resides in France.

"In Search of Maturin": Charles Maturin, novelist and playwright, best known for his gothic novel, *Melmoth the Wanderer*. Quotations are from his sermons and the Parish notebook, St. Peter's Parish, Dublin. Robert Emmet was hung drawn and quartered in Dublin for acts of rebellion in 1803.

"Eighty Butterfield Orchard": H block was the cell block in Long Kesh Prison, Northern Ireland where IRA prisoners and hunger strikers were housed.

"Broad St. Riots": The San Patricios were Irish deserters from the U.S. Army who served with Santa Anna's Mexican forces.

"The Connemarra Woman" is for my grandmother, Bab ap Anthony, Barbara McDonogh Gilboy, who posed for the titled painting by the Irish artist Charles Lamb when he summered in Carraroe, County Galway.

Praise for Kevin Bowen's first book of poetry,
Playing Basketball With the Veit Cong:

Chosen "Pick of the Year" by *The Progressive*

"*Playing Basketball with the Viet Cong* is surely one of the most
vibrant, most stirring, and most heart-breaking collections of
poetry to emerge from the Vietnam War. In rich, lucid language,
each line lovingly attended to, Kevin Bowen offers up indelible
images of both war and peace—the Vietnam of nightmare and
the Vietnam of waking reality. It is a beautiful book, one I'll
always treasure."
    —Tim O'Brien, author of *Going After Cacciato*, winner of
the National Book Award

"Beautiful. . . . Bowen captures the spirituality of Vietnam."
    —Oliver Stone

"Observant, honest, refined...and delicately brutal when it has
to be, *Playing Basketball with the Viet Cong* evocatively
suggests not only who we may have been then, but who we
might become."
    —*Manoa: A Pacific Journal of International Writing*

"It's only by reading books like *Playing Basketball With the Viet
Cong*, and by communicating with ourselves and others, that we
can begin or continue the healing process, and learn how to
transcend our memories through the Art of Forgiveness, both in
ourselves and in those we fought."
    —*Left Curve*

Kevin Bowen was drafted and served in the U.S. Army in the
Vietnam war during 1968-1969. He has since returned to
Vietnam numerous times and currently serves as Director of the
William Joiner Center Study of War and Social Consequences of
the University of Massachusetts at Boston. His first book,
Playing Basketball With the Viet Cong, was chosen as the **Pick
of the Year** by *The Progressive*. Bowen lives in Dorchester,
MA with his wife and two children.

CURBSTONE PRESS, INC.

is a nonprofit publishing house dedicated to literature that reflects a commitment to social change, with an emphasis on contemporary writing from Latin America and Latino communities in the United States. Curbstone presents writers who give voice to the unheard in a language that goes beyond denunciation to celebrate, honor and teach. Curbstone builds bridges between its writers and the public – from inner-city to rural areas, colleges to community centers, children to adults. Curbstone seeks out the highest aesthetic expression of the dedication to human rights and intercultural understanding: poetry, testimonials, novels, stories.

This mission requires more than just producing books. It requires ensuring that as many people as possible know about these books and read them. To achieve this, a large portion of Curbstone's schedule is dedicated to arranging tours and programs for its authors, working with public school and university teachers to enrich curricula, reaching out to underserved audiences by donating books and conducting readings and community programs, and promoting discussion in the media. It is only through these combined efforts that literature can truly make a difference.

Curbstone Press, like all non-profit presses, depends on the support of individuals, foundations, and government agencies to bring you, the reader, works of literary merit and social significance which might not find a place in profit-driven publishing channels, and to bring these writers into schools and communities across the country. Our sincere thanks to the many individuals who support this endeavor and to the following organizations, foundations and government agencies: Josef & Anni Albers Foundation, Witter Bynner Foundation for Poetry, Connecticut Commission on the Arts, Connecticut Arts Endowment Fund, Connecticut Humanities Council, Ford Foundation, Lawson Valentine Foundation, LEF Foundation, Lila Wallace-Reader's Digest Fund, The Open Society Institute, The Andrew W. Mellon Foundation, National Endowment for the Arts, the Puffin Foundation and the Samuel Rubin Foundation.

Please support Curbstone's efforts to present the diverse voices and views that make our culture richer. Tax-deductible donations can be made by check or credit card to Curbstone Press, 321 Jackson Street, Willimantic, CT 06226   Tel: (860) 423-5110.